IELTS WRITING TASK 2 SAMPLES

Over 45 High-Quality Model Essays for Your Reference to Gain a High Band Score 8.0+ In 1 Week (Book 13)

RACHEL MITCHELL

ISBN: 9781973260493

TEXT COPYRIGHT © [RACHEL MITCHELL]

TABLE OF CONTENT

INTRODUCTION

Thank you and congratulate you for downloading the book *"IELTS Writing Task 2 Samples: Over 45 High Quality Model Essays for Your Reference to Gain a High Band Score 8.0+ In 1 Week (Book 13)."*

This book is well designed and written by an experienced native teacher from the USA who has been teaching IELTS for over 10 years. She really is the expert in training IELTS for students at each level. In this book, she will provide you over 45 high quality model essays to help you easily achieve an 8.0+ in the IELTS Writing Task 2, even if your English is not excellent. These samples will also walk you through step-by-step on how to develop your well-organized answers for the Task 2 Writing.

As the author of this book, I believe that this book will be an indispensable reference and trusted guide for you who may want to maximize your band score in IELTS task 2 writing. Once you read this book, I guarantee you that you will have learned an extraordinarily wide range of useful, and practical IELTS WRITING TASK 2 model essays that will help you become a successful IELTS taker as well as you will even become a successful English writer in work and in life within a short period of time only.

Take action today and start getting better scores tomorrow!

Thank you again for purchasing this book, and I hope you enjoy it.

SAMPLE 1

Some people believe that studying at university or college is the best route to a successful career, which others believe that it is better to get a job straight after school. Discuss both sides and give your opinion.

It is true that many people choose to pursue tertiary education after graduating from high school to achieve an academic qualification. Whereas some would argue that work after high school education is the best choice to obtain a successful career. However, I personally believe that attending university significantly contributes to professional achievement.

On the one hand, there are several reasons why a lot of school leavers choose to embark on a career right after graduation. Firstly, many believe that getting real-life experience and the knowledge from jobs may be a better preparation to obtain the future employment. Supposing an employee working in marketing office often has to handle different or even unpredictable situations from their customers or suppliers. These experiences partly teach how to solve problems flexibly and be responsible for the job with others, and especially help them establish essential habits and skills which contribute to the future career. Secondly, working after high school arms young adults with a taste of what a career in a particular industry might be like. As a result, this helps make a more informed decision on what they want to do over the long haul.

On the other hand, the beneficial impact that university education brings to youngsters is undeniable. They believe that universities help them enlighten their vision, expand domain, and polish skills. For instance, teenagers are able to develop significant skills such as time management, teamwork, even leadership skills as well as promote their strength. Obviously, these essential skills will be obtained thanks to various activities during university life such as planning research, working a part-time job or taking part in extra curriculum activities. Therefore, attending university or college ensures not only their education but the development of their future career as well.

In conclusion, there are convincing arguments both for and against pursuing higher education. However, I strongly believe that studying at universities is the logical and best option.

319 words

SAMPLE 2

Some people think that spending a lot on holding wedding parties, birthday parties, and other celebrations is just a waste of money. Others, however, think that these are necessary for individuals and the society.

Discuss both views and give your opinion.

Some people believe that it is not a big deal to spend a lot of money on celebrations while those who oppose this idea believe that costly celebrations are wasteful. I would argue that spending money on holding these parties offers more advantages than disadvantages.

On the one hand, it is beneficial to invest a great amount of money on special events related to some public relations and private reasons. Firstly, pricey celebrations are the common ways to symbolize a person's social status. It is true that a few people can afford an expensive party, the more you pay the wealthier you are. If a famous businessman holds a luxury event, it can enhance his image and reputation as the party draws the considerable attention of the public which is beneficial for his business. Secondly, high – priced events can bring people joys. It is undeniable that a wedding is considered as the most important day in a person's life and their families love to have a fancy time together. That is the main reason why they invest time and money in a luxury ceremony with an extravagant set of menu prepared and a famous band playing during the ceremony. For instance, a top-rated restaurant would hold a flawless wedding night to make it memorable for all the guests due to their professional service.

On the other hand, it is true to some extent that wasting money on these events is unnecessary. Many people are pushed beyond their financial capabilities in order to meet all demands and fulfill the wishes of others. The major result is that they have to face debts and financial burdens later on which leads to financial-related anxieties.

In conclusion, while holding luxury events is wasteful at times, it seems to me that the advantages of celebrating fancy celebrations outweigh the drawbacks.

305 words

SAMPLE 3

Life was better when technology was simpler. To what extent do you agree or disagree?

People have different views about whether technology makes human life better or not. From my perspective, while I admit that there are some problems stemming from technology, I concur with those who believe that advantages in technology have brought a lot of benefits to mankind, making our life much easier/ more convenient.

On the one hand, modern technology plays a crucial role in our daily life in modern times, helping us to do almost everything faster and giving us more chances to relax. Firstly, just having some basic skills in computers or smartphones, people can exchange information or text messages instantly by using email or social networking like Facebook or Twitter. Without technology, this certainly will take people enormous time. Secondly, with the invention of mp3, mp4 players such as Ipad, Ipod, and people now can listen to music, watch movies everywhere whenever they have free time to relieve stress and make their life more colorful.

On the other hand, some people, especially the old generation, argue that technology is too complicated. The big reason is that not all senior citizens are 'silver-surfers' so some gadgets are not easy for them to use. Thus, some sophisticated software being installed in these high-tech devices require the amount of time and passion to explore them that might be suitable for the youngsters. Another reason is that people now are over-reliant on technology in their work as well as their personal life. For example, most of their important data store in computers, if someone hacks and gets their information, they might lose a lot.

In conclusion, although there are strong arguments for both views, I strongly believe technology is truly life-saver, bringing many positive merits in comparison with its harmful impacts on our life.

291 words

SAMPLE 4

In the future, it seems it will be more difficult to live in the Earth. Some people think more money should be spent on researching other planets to live, such as Mars. To what extent do you agree or disagree with this statement?

It is true that in the future, it will be more and more difficult for humans to sustain on Earth. Therefore, some people argue that resources should be spent to find new planets to settle in. Personally, I agree with this idea and I believe that people have all means to achieve it.

There are two primary reasons why life on Earth is becoming more insecure and unsustainable. One important reason is the potential danger of nuclear radiation has threatened the existence of humans since it was used for the first time in Hiroshima and Nagasaki and killed thousands of people. Today, nine countries in the world own nuclear weapons, especially North Korea with the increasing tests of nuclear missiles to counteract against the US. The prospect of world war III among powerful countries with destructive weapons would be the end of mankind. Another strong reason is the rising level of pollution has intensely ruined the ecosystem and (has) degraded the quality of life. For example, in Vietnam, tons of industrial rubbish have been released illegally into the ocean, causing the mass fish deaths and destroying aquatic life.

However, seeking for livable planets beyond the Earth is a bold idea but worthy and is encouraged by many potential advantages. Firstly, the development of astronomy enables mankind to explore new planets far beyond the solar system. Hopefully, in the near future, scientists will discover planets with a similar structure with the Earth. Secondly, with the proliferation of technology, hundreds of spaceships and space stations have been put into orbit to help humans conquest space. Nowadays, space tourism is no longer an impractical idea when companies like SpaceX offers an adventure to the lunar by commercial spaceships.

In conclusion, as the degradation of the Earth is a vital problem of all human, the quest for a new homeland in the universe is extremely essential and I strongly believe that mankind has all resources to conduct it.

324 words

SAMPLE 5

Discuss the advantages and disadvantages of playing sports and participating in physical exercises.

It is undeniable that people of all ages should take up exercises regularly to have a good health and keep their body in good shape. I am of the opinion that there are more benefits of this trend than the disadvantages.

There are both mentally and physically considerable benefits to engage in playing/ taking part in sports games. Firstly, being athletic can avoid obesity which represents a major public health concern. Fat is burnt and excessive calories are shed through rigorous physical activity involved in sports. In fact, people who regularly play sports stay healthy and positively than those do not. Secondly, sport is an effective stress reliever by drawing your concentration toward your activity and away from other responsibilities. To be more specific, when participating in a sports game, you focus on your body's movements instead of other depression and anxiety. According to HuffPost, people who regularly participate in doing exercises can lower levels of stress more than non-athletic ones.

On the other hand, participating physical exercises carries possible health risks and injuries. The main problem is that you will get a high probability of injury during playing sports if you start exercise without proper preparation and clear instruction. Without the prior session before playing sports, muscle is not activated enough and easily broken down when lifting heavy weights. Moreover, an investment in a gymnastic course and sports facilities is frequently unaffordable to middle-class. In developing countries, participating in sports is costly and considered as an upper-class activity while many people get troubles with means of livelihood to support themselves and their family.

In conclusion, the merits of taking up sports or physical exercises outweigh the drawbacks as they exert positive influences on the mental and physical health of the player. Thus, everyone should always take risks into consideration to reap the benefits of such activities.

307 words

SAMPLE 6

Some people work for the same organization all their working life. Others think that it is better to work for different organizations. Discuss both these views and give your own opinion.

Career choice is one of the most important decisions in someone's life. While some people tend to be loyal to one company for their whole life, others choose to experience different environments by working for more than one employer. In my point of view, both trends bring its own advantages and drawbacks; however, I am more convinced by the latter one.

First, working a permanent job guarantee a stable life. It is obvious that when attempts are put in just one place, achievements are always the most worthwhile. Thanks to their long-term dedication, an employee is more likely to be assigned to an important position. In Vietnam, this choice is often made by people who want to become employees of national organizations in order to be entitled stable career yet with slow development and sometimes low salary. Other advantages perhaps include firm relations with colleagues and bosses, ultimate focus on solely a major or high social position in life as well. However, this career choice may results in depression and discouragement due to job's repetition. This would lead to giving up and losing goals in life if one is not consistent enough.

On the other hand, developing a career in various places allows young people to be exposed to a wide range of environments which enables them to further develop interpersonal skills. Without a doubt, youngsters are assigned different tasks requiring them to use different skills and giving them a chance of obtaining knowledge of various majors to build up broader knowledge. Moreover, the wide social network is also a plus as workers have an opportunity to interact with different counterparts and form great relations/ build strong relationships. Nevertheless, one would find this working style temporary as it guarantees no sustainability in the long term and workers hardly get a promotion or climb to a high position as they tend to leave the job before they get any.

In conclusion, as a youngster, I find the latter choice more thrilling due to its flexibility and activeness. However, the former choice would more suitable to those who'd rather want to settle down and have a lifetime career.

330 words

SAMPLE 7

In many countries, more and more people choose to buy imported food rather than produced locally. Why people buy imported food? What could be done to encourage people to buy local food?

A majority of people in the modern world prefer purchasing foreign foods rather than domestic products. There are some reasons and suggested solutions to tackle this problem.

Three essential causes below are listed as the explanation for why more and more local residents abandon their area's foods. Firstly, it is an indisputable fact that imported food has higher quality. Each item is checked and preserved carefully before delivering, which creates the loyalty as well as the preference from customers. Secondly, in the busy life, people tend to shop at supermarkets, where imported foods are omnipresent ranging from vegetables like herbs to high- quality fruits. Therefore, they cannot avoid choosing them. Finally, local food has existed for years, and consumers might be too familiar with them. In addition, as having a significant rise in the average income of citizens, expensive items become affordable to people.

Some measures should be taken to help local products obtain their position again. The most important action is to diversify all present products proactively and follow the world's trend. When prevailing agricultural products have existed, consumers would be willing to get them instead of buying foreign foods. Moreover, governments in some countries should give their hands in overcoming the shortages of the local business environment such as reducing indoor taxes and raising imported food taxes or having a campaign which stimulates citizen's consuming behaviors. On top of that, consumers themselves should be more aware of the fact that some food items produced in foreign countries are processed with modified generation technology.

In conclusion, people in many countries prefer to buy foreign food because of some clear reasons, therefore, several solutions should be considered to encourage local residents to come back using food that produced locally.

289 words

SAMPLE 8

Some people argue that demands for public services and facilities are ever-increasing in today's fast-paced society and should be top of the government's agenda. I only agree with the notion to an extent, believing that art has its redeeming features that cannot be overlooked.

On the one hand, investment from governments into public sectors can bring numerous benefits in terms of the augmented transportation system and improved living conditions for individuals. With regard to the former, through the subsidies granted by the states, effectively designed and properly maintained road systems can be facilitated, which is a fundamental contributor to a well-functioned and free-flowing traffic system. This could lead to reductions in traffic jams, traffic congestions along with declines in accidents taking place on the streets and, in turn, results in massive time saved and efficiency boosted for road users. The second benefit is that projects relating to public domains add significant values to people's lives by accommodating communities' basic needs via establishing parks, commercial centers, schools, to name but a few. The citizens who find their needs and desires comprehensively and painstakingly catered for by the government are more likely to enjoy their lives to a greater extent whereas developing a higher level of trust in the government.

Aside from the aforementioned arguments, I am of the opinion that arts play an indispensable role in life and merit equal attention and financial funding. The reason is if considered carefully, especially in juxtaposition to other needs, art does not pale in its significance in fostering a healthy and productive workforce. A case in point is that going to the cinema, visiting art exhibitions, watching live concerts or participating in other art-related activities with friends or family can produce a sense of relaxation and release stress, which is necessitated by overwhelming workloads at hectic workplaces.

In conclusion, although there are obvious advantages from investing in the public services and amenities, I would argue that more attention should be paid to arts as to maintain a work-life balance.

330 words

SAMPLE 9

In the modern world, there is a movement away from written exams to more practical assessment.

Discuss the advantages and disadvantages of this trend.

Nowadays, more and more corporations and universities have applied new methods such as practical assessments, particularly speaking tests or debating tests instead of traditional exams. They believe that those changes can assist the enterprises to look for talented and appropriate staff effectively.

There is no doubt that practical assessments are highly trusted to evaluate candidates precisely based on the reality that they bring. For example, the contesters have to handle the hands-on challenges with examiners who directly interview them. Therefore, the consideration has come to be general thanks to not only the knowledge but also the manner, interaction, traits, social skills or communication. In addition to this, these modifications on the evaluating processes also encourage the young generation to focus more on the issues of society than concentrating on specific fields of their life.

On the other hand, I strongly believe that there still exist demerits that practical tests have not been resolved yet. It is easy to indicate that estimating the ability of human beings based on practical examinations tends to be subjective and apparently is unfair to all individuals. By contrast, the traditional tests like multiple choices have guaranteed the justice via benchmarking that has been published or announced popularly, although evaluation could not be always accurate.

In conclusion, there are some drawbacks to practical tests. If they have been spreading out, it seems to me that they are more beneficial for the society and the community in looking for a large number of talented people for nations in a comprehensive development.

254 words

SAMPLE 10

Some people think that all teenagers should be required to do unpaid work in their free time to help the local community. They believe this would benefit both the individual teenager and society as a whole.

Do you agree or disagree?

Many people hold the belief that young students ought to compulsorily do unsalaried work which might lead to positive impacts on themselves as well as the society. While there are some obviously good points to do volunteer activities, I believe that teenagers' willingness also needs to be taken into consideration rather than forcing them to do regardless of their opinions.

On the one hand, it is obviously beneficial for students to do take part in charity works. Firstly, they are able to get some working experiences by participating in unpaid tasks which could be valuable for their resume when applying for their future education or career. Secondly, a variety of volunteer activities including helping the elderly, disabled people or cleaning city streets or delivering food to underprivileged people teach them how to take care those who are in need or how to support people with difficulties. These soft skills will play a very important role in their lives. Also throughout these activities, the youth can hopefully be more mature and have more responsibility to not only their own lives but only the people around them.

At the same time, I believe that if young students are forced to do these kinds of unpaid tasks, they are reluctant to do and it might cause the bad results or even can lead to their negative attitude towards volunteer work. Another point should be noted is that students nowadays are under pressure of extensive curriculum at school, thus they are deserved to have free time to relax or enjoy their hobbies rather than requiring them to do no-paid work.

In conclusion, it is better to allow students to choose activities based on their preference in their spare time in steads of forcing all of them to unpaid work.

295 words

SAMPLE 11

Some people think that government should take measures regarding the healthy lifestyle of individuals. Others think it must be managed by individuals. Discuss both sides and give your opinion.

There are lots of contrasting views about how healthy lifestyle needs to be controlled. According to some, health care is determined by the government, whilst many argue that individuals need to be responsible for their lifestyle. Personally, I believe that healthy lifestyle should be a choice of each person.

On the one hand, it is thought that the government should apply restricted measures to ensure citizens' healthy lifestyle. There is no doubt that health care of citizens is a preference and has contributed enormously to the social growth. Moreover, to ensure the physical and mental health, some policies such as subsidizing health food for the poor and imposing heavy taxes on unhealthy food need to be formulated by the countries government. Besides, some well- equipped sports facilities also should be built and expanded in various areas, aiming at physical health development. Consequently, the government's actions are beneficial to citizens' welfare state.

The significant role of the government towards citizen's health cannot be denied, however, some anti- advocates believe that the healthy lifestyle should be decided by individuals. In fact, each of us has different choices and the habit of a healthy life. More importantly, no one can comprehend our own life as much as we can and how we often keep being healthy on a daily basis. For instance, when someone catches diseases such as flu, fatigue or even cancer, they can overcome and heal those illnesses because they understand what diet or nutrient is the best for their health.

In conclusion, I strongly believed that each individual should apply appropriate approaches to health care in their daily basis, while the government of a country needs to guarantee proper treatment and facilities for a healthy lifestyle.

286 words

SAMPLE 12

Some people think that school should reward students who show the best academic results, while others believe that it is more important to reward students who show improvements. Discuss both views and give your own opinion.

Nowadays, the question of whether to reward students based on their academic results or improvements still remains as a source of controversy. While a number of people believe that schools should recognize the best student's achievements, I am of the opinion that praising their improvements is more plausible.

On the one hand, there are a couple of reasons for rewarding students' grades. Firstly, this could create a highly competitive environment, which might urge all students in a class to try hard as possible to get the best scores. Indeed, being praised in front of the class could be a fulfilling moment for each student and encourages the others to make a greater attempt next time. Secondly, through rewarding the best achievements, the gifted students are identified, so they can be given more attention to nurturing their abilities. For example, each school always chooses some certain advanced students to improve their capabilities aiming to participate in national competitions.

On the other hand, I would argue that giving encouragements for those who make a great process is more equitable. The first benefit would be all students can have an equal chance to receive rewards. Instead of feeling disappointed for not attaining a high score in a test, students who show significant headways all deserve to be honored, which leads to the fact that all students need to try hard in a long-term period of time rather than focusing on just exams. Another benefit is that learning without worrying about grades could bring in enjoyment and understanding. Besides, when the main aim of education is knowledge-gaining, not high-score achieving, the exam pressure will be reduced and the cheating for high marks will no longer remain the big concern for education.

In conclusion, even though rewarding a student with the highest scores could be beneficial to some extents, it seems to me that it is more important to recognize the improvements of the individual.

320 words

SAMPLE 13

New technologies have changed the way children spend their free time. Do advantages of this outweigh disadvantages?

It is true that many children nowadays are spending a large amount of spare time playing with modern technological devices. While it might have some drawbacks in some ways, I believe that benefits are more considerable.

On the one hand, there are a couple of disadvantages for children when they abuse technological gadgets. Firstly, getting addicted to modern devices could lead to the lack of time spent on communication and interaction between a child and his or her parents, so some mental problems might arise. Indeed, autism now is one of the most common disorders among children, which results from receiving less care and attention from other members of a family. Secondly, sticking to the screens for hours to play games on smartphones or computers might leads to an unhealthy condition for most youngsters which results from the deficient amount of time for exercises, such as obesity.

On the other hand, I would argue that the latest technologies bring to children lots of more benefits than drawbacks. One reason for this view is that kids can broaden their knowledge through using interactive softwares. For example, they can not only learn English with the assistance of useful apps on smartphones, but also obtain valuable information through educational programs such as discovery or science channels. Furthermore, through a long period of time accessing and playing modern pieces of equipment, kids can figure out whether working with them is their passion or not. If parents find out the children' enthusiasm for technologies, it could be a good time to gradually nurture their passion by guiding them to use these things in a right way.

In conclusion, it seems to me that the potential advantages regarding children spending time for latest technologies are more significant than the possible drawbacks.

295 words

SAMPLE 14

The animal species are becoming extinct due to human activities on land and in the sea.

What are the reasons and solutions?

It is true that an increasing number of species has been on the verge of extinction for current centuries. This problem is believed to originate from a wide range of human activities. Therefore, people should definitely propose sufficient steps to tackle this phenomenon.

To begin with, there would be three main reasons in human responsibilities for animal extinction. Firstly, land invading for agriculture and accommodation has been damaging natural habitats. For example, large areas of forest are destroyed as a consequence of human involvement, which leads to potential disasters that occur and kill rare animals. Secondly, numerous poison sources from industrial zone and daily activities' waste products also contaminate the environment, in which many extinct animals are living. Finally, overexploitation and illegal huntings are noticeable to contribute the decrease of species' population. Especially, people utilize bombs, electricity and dangerous equipment to catch fish in large sea areas, so that it will not only lead species to die unreasonably but also put potentially harms on the local residents.

However, it is vital to take action to solve this problem right away. On the top priority, the government should immediately impose a ban on hunting and consuming rare animals. This is believed to raise people's awareness of the importance of rare species. Apart from that, more public sites should be constructed to preserve and protect them from dangers. It is necessary to recreate natural habitats for breeding various kinds of animals. Moreover, we should encourage other people to use recycling products in term of reducing the amount of waste garbage. Last but not least, environmental-polluting factories have to be fined heavily on what they have done to the nature.

In conclusion, many animals will be urged to the extinction unless there are no effective measures allocated to negative impacts of human on rare species. Anyways, each individual should make efforts to improve the wildlife environment, as well as the way our industrialization develops.

321 words

SAMPLE 15

It is neither possible nor useful for a country to provide places for a high proportion of young people. To what extent do you agree or disagree?

Education undoubtedly plays an integral part in the society, contributing to the development of a country. However, recently it has been said that as the number of young people is on the rise, providing university places for them is neither possible nor useful. Personally, I do not totally agree with this opinion.

On the one hand, I admittedly agree that there is no likelihood to provide fully-equipped places of tertiary education for all the young, especially in developing countries. One obvious obstacle those governments are facing is the lack of financial support. In fact, in many areas, the local authorities do not even have enough budget to build a primary school, let alone a tertiary institution. Another problem that should be noted is that due to a booming population, not every university has enough space and qualified infrastructure facilities to meet the demand of the mounting number of students. Take Vietnam National University for example, the administration of the university used to hire rooms in other places which had a higher capacity to provide places for students attending lectures.

On the other hand, it is always useful for the young to experience the academic environment, because the society as a whole certainly benefits from that. Firstly, if young people were provided with a chance of education, the economic gap between regions would be reduced, because it would offer the young generation equal opportunities to identify and develop their careers, bringing about the prosperity of their countries. Another similarly important point is that a university is an ideal place for young people to hone their theoretical and practical skills. With constant interaction with their lecturers and peers, they definitely have every chance to broaden their view of life and enhancing their social relationship. From another perspective, the government is nurturing the country's future workforce in an educational atmosphere.

In conclusion, although not always possible, it is still useful to reserve university places for all the young.

325 words

SAMPLE 16

Some people think that in this modern world people are getting dependent on each other, while others think the modern world gets people more independent on each other. Discuss both views and give your own opinion.

It is widely argued that people are becoming more reliant on others, as opposed to others who believe that people are more independent in the modern society. While each view has its own reasons, my perspective is that independence has been more emphasized in this progressive world.

To begin with, some people may become more dependent on others. One main reason is that the majority of people rely on food produced by others. While our ancestors tended to plant and supply food by themselves, the majority of citizens are reliant on food produced by companies. For instance, KFC, which is a fast food company, has been growing swiftly in recent years to meet the increasing need for fast foods from people living in urban areas. If the production of food is insufficient, numerous people will not be able to produce food on their own to satisfy their demands.

In spite of the aforementioned point, my view is that people are more independent in modern time. First and foremost, families in many countries are becoming smaller and more dispersed. People are now capable of travelling to other nations easily and living far from their family. For example, students in this modern world have the opportunities to study abroad, so they will have to live independently from their parents. Secondly, the liberty of people has been prioritized in modern society hence each individual can freely express their ideas and thoughts without being influenced by authorities.

To conclude, while it is certainly true that people become more reliant in some aspects, I hold the belief that each person is more independent in this modern society.

272 words

SAMPLE 17

The old generations often hold traditional ideas about the correct way of life, thinking and behavior. However, some people think that these ideas are not helpful for young people to prepare for modern life. To what extent do you agree or disagree?

It is true that many older people believe in traditional values that often seem incompatible with the needs of younger people. While I agree that some traditional ideas are outdated, I believe that others are still useful and should not be forgotten.

I accept that there are some beliefs, especially for males such as male-dominated thoughts which are inappropriate in today's world and needs to be changed. Due to this idea, women have no opportunity to enjoy fundamental rights that every male could have easily, such as to go to school or to be an heiress. That limits women's abilities and they could not do anything to show themselves though, actually, their talents are as wonderful as male's.

Despite that, I still think some traditional ideas should be preserved and developed due to the positive effects they could give and the most integral benefit they could do, in my opinion, is to help to protect and develop the national identity. The traditional thoughts are a part of the culture and they make the difference between each nation. If a nation could not preserve its own character, it would be in unsustainable development and citizens living in that would not understand who they are, what their beauties are and what the wonderful things they deserve, and further, they might be not confident with thought that what they own is worse than foreign residents'.

In conclusion, it is not true that all traditional thoughts are not helpful, and some of them should be rejected because they are not suitable for modern life but some should be preserved and developed for sustainable national development.

271 words

SAMPLE 18

Some people say that parents should control their children's behavior from a very young age. What do you think?

Shaping children's personality/ value when they are very young plays a vital role in their future. Thus, some people hold the belief that children's manner ought to be under strict supervision. I strongly agree with this view because of the following reasons.

On the one hand, young people are very vulnerable and easily influenced by grave things. It is undeniable that the cutting-edge technology and many innovative inventions enable children to access the great source of information through mobile phones or television. However, some movies and websites have not been censored and they may contain violent and unsuitable/ inappropriate content for children. These things will have a detrimental effect on children's behavior because they quickly imitate what they see. Therefore, if there is no intermediate intervention on time, this will result in several serious/ detrimental consequences for children's future.

On the other hand, at the early stage of life, children are usually immature to be able to differentiate between right and wrong. They may unintentionally do something without knowing the consequence of it. For example, a student stole a little amount of money from his friend and he thought that it was a joke. However, it was a wrong behavior and in some cases, and it could be considered illegal in which he has to be punished. Therefore, adults had better have control over children's manner in order to make sure that they do appropriate actions.

In conclusion, parents should impose strict supervision on their children's behavior because they are easily affected by bad things and not aware of what is right and wrong. I think that this is one of the best ways to prevent children from badly behaving and guide them to be a good citizen when they are young.

292 words

SAMPLE 19

In many educational institutions, there is a tendency that female students choose/ prefer art-related subjects while their male counterparts are fond of science ones. There are certainly several reasons for this trend which I believe should remain unchanged.

There are a variety of reasons for this trend. One underlying justification is the innate ability of each gender which decides what subjects they are good at. Specifically, organizational skills and logical thinking, which are necessary requirements for working in the scientific field, are outstanding masculine traits. Whereas, it is believed that most females possess a good sense of creativity and concept of beauty, which accounts for their advantage in major concerning arts. Another reason for this is based on their personal preference. There is mounting evidence that since they are knee-high to a grasshopper, boys enjoy playing with robots and watching science-fiction movies, while girls prefer dressing their dolls up and cooking games.

I believe this tendency of subject options among boys and girls is a natural development that should not be altered. If their parents try to make the change against their will when they are children, it may, more or less, have negative impacts on their development in terms of mentality later in their life. However, such trend is not always the case. There are still boys with excellent style of design and girls with logical ability outstripped their male peers. In both cases, the optimal recommendation is to let young people freely identify their advantages/ strength as well as passion and nurture them.

In conclusion, the trend of girls choosing arts and boys opting for science in schools and universities are easily understandable and it seems to me that people should let that trend go with the natural course.

291 words

SAMPLE 20

People tend to live alone or in small family units rather than extended family

Discuss the advantages and disadvantages of this trend.

In the past, it is common for two or three generations living together in one family. However, an increasing number of people prefer living alone or in the nuclear family to extended one. This essay will take both the advantages and disadvantages into consideration.

There are surely many benefits when people live alone or in a small family. First, at all, this allows people to have more freedom and comfort. To be more specific, they do not need to ask for permission of their parents whilst going home late or they can freely decorate their own room according to their preference. Secondly, living alone brings them an independent life as they may take care of themselves and know how to control the time as well as their budget. Last but not least, people can enjoy their privacy and peace when they live alone or in a nuclear family. In fact, there is not much noise at all so they are not able to achieve higher working productivity and better job performance when they get enough relaxation.

However, there are several difficulties that people may have to deal with when living separately. Above all, the loneliness is the problem which they have to face. Not only does nobody give them a hand when they need support but no one also shares their joy and sorrow. Besides, they may not have a lot of opportunities to visit grandparents or relatives so the family ties/ bonds are not much strong. It is also difficult for them to take care of the elder when not living under the one roof. Finally, there is no help from grandparents to look after grandchildren as well as cannot share the housework or accommodation together.

In conclusion, the advantages and disadvantages always exist equally/ parallel when people do not live with more generations or just only themselves.

309 words

SAMPLE 21

Economic progress is one factor that is being considered to measure the success of a country, but there are other factors that should be considered when measuring the success of a country. Do you agree or disagree? What other factors do you think should be considered? Do you think one factor is more important than others?

One of the most heated controversy issues today relates to economic growth. Many citizens claim that although economy can play an important role to guarantee the prosperity of a nation, there are other progresses which should be taken into consideration. Personally, I strongly agree with this viewpoint as/ because of the following reasons.

On the one hand, I certainly believe that economy is one of the most crucial keys to raise the position of the countries on an international scale. Indeed, when owning a healthy economy, the local authorities definitely attract many rich investors and is are becoming increasingly popular all around the world. This advantage will make some worthy contributions to create more opportunities for residents to seek a top job with a strong income. Therefore, it helps many people improve the standard of living such as being taken care of by essential medical care and having a chance to study at top-tier universities.

On the other hand, I also think that other factors can foster the development of a country such as the environment and education. It is undeniable that the advance of the economy is possibly meaningless if the public community has no an awareness of the importance of natural habitat. For example, although governments can receive a lot of money from industrial factories, they really have to allocate more funds to refresh polluted air and water. Besides, the good education will help a lot of students enrich their mind as well as limit the number of crimes every year. This positive factor possibly brings a peaceful life with a positive atmosphere to live and work.

From what has been discussed above, one can reach a conclusion that both economy and other aspects have an essential role for the survival of a country.

296 words

SAMPLE 22

Some universities offer online courses as an alternative to classes delivered on campus. Do you think this is a positive or negative development?

It is true that education is the key to success and also a right that should be entitled to everyone. Recently, some universities have started to provide online education instead of face-to-face courses. I believe this is a positive innovation in the educational system.

On the one hand, there is no denying that direct lectures on campus are the most common form of education which has certain advantages. First and foremost, it provides an academic atmosphere that fosters a sense of discipline among students. Secondly, their academic performance is likely to improve notably thanks to the constant interaction with lecturers. Lastly, they can possibly enhance their social relationship by communicating with their peers. However, such form of education is not always available for everyone, which is the reason that lies behind the creation of online courses.

On the other hand, distant learning offers everyone an equal access to education. Not only people in urban areas but also fulltime employees and residents in remote places can experience the up-to-standard academic environment. Additionally, they are provided with a cost-effective mode of learning, because without the cost of hiring or purchasing the educational facilities, the prices for such courses are fairly reasonable.

Similarly important is that online education gives students more control over their schedule, which facilitates the balance between study and recreational activities. It should also be noted that with a flexible timetable, students definitely have more time to gain real-life experience by seeking a job, whether full-time or part-time. In this sense, there is every likelihood that they will be fully-equipped with necessary skills by the time of graduation, consequently, have a good start on their career path.

In conclusion, I believe that online academic courses offered by some universities will certainly make a great contribution to the global education.

299 words

SAMPLE 23

Report research suggests that majority of criminals who were sent to prison would commit crimes when they are set free. What do you think of this case? What to be done to solve this problem?

It is argued that prisoners tend to commit crimes again after they reintegrate back into the society. While there are a number of causes of this, many measures can be taken to deal with the situation.

There are two primary reasons why people turn to crime again. Firstly, the imprisoned time makes it hard for people to reintegrate back into the society. Things change every day, and that they may feel strange and scared of embarking on new aspects of their life. Therefore, criminals will trace back to the non-lethal way as it is familiar and helps to supply them the comfort. Another reason is that the full weight of the law is not implemented seriously. For example, in my country, people who are under 18 years old will not suffer the capital punishment despite their serious crimes. That justifies why the crime rate among youngsters is increasing.

However, the governments and each individual can take actions to solve this problem. Governments should impose some policies to raise criminals' awareness of serious laws and different types of punishments. As a result, they can accumulate sufficient knowledge of the measures and try to avoid turning to crimes again. Most importantly, the government should provide them with jobs/ vocational training and good condition to improve the standard of living as well as motivate hidden talented people who can be attributed to the development/ prosperity of the nation in various fields.

All in all, although the issue is considered extremely serious, there are many ways to tackle it, helping the prisons become law-abiding citizens.

261 words

SAMPLE 24

Some people argue that providing assistance to all people in need around the world is beyond the bonds of the possibility of any government. Therefore, the governments should only give priority to the citizens of their own countries. Personally, I disagree with this view.

The first reason is that the proliferation of transportation enables us to provide international aid quickly and sufficiently. The modern means of transport allows government agencies and international bodies bring the assistance to people who need in even relatively remote areas of the world. There have been a number of recent examples of how government support can help in time to recover the damage of unfortunate people. Last year, in Butan – an inaccessible country located in the Himalaya mountain range, the country recorded the most devastating earthquake which deprived the life of hundreds of innocent people and also left thousands of others homeless in desperate need of food and shelter. Unhesitatingly, the response of governments around the world brought an enormous amount of supplies, including food and tents by skyways, and medical staff also volunteered to help injured people.

Another reason is that I think we are living in the same world, sharing the same home, despite our different living places, we have a moral responsibility to give a helping hand to underprivileged people. International relief organizations like UNICEF or the Red Cross were established to remind us of our international obligations towards suffering people in our world. These duties cannot be placed only on any single organizations but with the support of all countries, more people will be helped to overcome the tragedy. Therefore, the governments need to support international aid bodies with both effort and materials.

In conclusion, it is true that government must not ignore the urgent matter in their own countries. But I believe that we have the means and responsibilities to help everyone in need regardless of the separation of geographical boundaries.

321 words

SAMPLE 25

Aircrafts have been increasingly used to transport fruits and vegetables to some countries where such plants hardly grow or are out of season. Some people consider it a good trend, but some people oppose it. Discuss both views and give your opinion.

There is a significant rise recently in airplane use for the delivery service of fruits and vegetables. Many people hold the belief that importing agricultural products by air freight is good whereas others disagree. I totally agree with the former view.

On the one hand, using aircrafts to transport fruits and vegetables is beneficial in two important ways. Firstly, the government can effectively implement specification strategy for different areas with specific features. While industrial zones in which farming is not suitable, rural areas provide agricultural products based on their geographic advantages. Only by this way can we make the most of the available resources to maximize profits with minimum costs. Secondly, thanks to advances in technology, the airplane has long been a popular means of transport in terms of its high speed. Hence, agricultural products can be transported easily from one place to the others within hours. Besides, with the specific storage of goods, airplanes can maintain fruits and vegetables fresh over long-haul air flights. For instance, due to high demand for fresh imported cherries, there is a massive growth in shipments by air freight in China.

On the other hand, using aircrafts to transport fruits and vegetables has the environmental drawback. To begin with, air pollution rate has been increasing in step with the widespread use of airplanes. In fact, plane exhaust contains a variety of air pollutants, including sulfur dioxide and nitrogen oxides. This leads to respiratory diseases, including lung cancer.

In a nutshell, I would say that importing agricultural products by aircrafts has both merits and demerits, but the pros outweigh the cons.

266 words

SAMPLE 26

It is neither possible nor useful for a country to provide university places for a high proportion of young people. To what extent do you agree or disagree?

It is true that furnishing the young generations with tertiary education plays an indispensable part in the government's policies. However, mostly the policy makers reckon that it is infeasible and inefficient to offer the vast majority higher education. From my perspective, I am completely convinced with this statement for/ because of the following reasons.

It proves impossible for a country to provide higher education for all young people/ youngsters. The first reason is the prohibitive tuition fee and the inability/ the shortage of financial ability to afford the majority of youths. Generally, colleges and university undergraduates are supposed to purchase costly materials, let alone the field trips in many disciplines like engineering and medicine. All of these reveal the fact that many students from rural areas find it fairly tough to meet annual house-renting fee as well as tuition fee, especially in poverty-stricken countries. Besides, there are other priorities the government should take into consideration, such as healthcare system and charity.

It also does not seem useful for the whole country to state wish to accommodate the youth with university places. This is primarily because there is no guarantee that all university students will become successful enough to contribute to the prosperity of the nation. There are numerous cases when distinguished graduates cannot find/ seek decent jobs, they will exacerbate the financial burden on their family and the society; as a consequence, this raises the thought that tertiary education is subsidized or free of charge.

In conclusion, it is my firm belief that it is neither possible nor useful for a country to provide a vast majority of young adults with university education access.

274 words

SAMPLE 27

In the modern time, it is true that English is gaining more and more popularity on its way to become an international language. While there are strong arguments in support of both sides of this phenomenon, I am of the opinion that the benefits offered by the upsurge in English usage will keep overwhelming its downsides.

First of all, there is no doubt about the benefits of using English as an international language. To begin with, English is one of the most powerful means of communication. By having a global language, not only can we get to know people in our country but also expand our circle of acquaintances to other nations. On top of it, the widespread of English also acts as an effective way to alleviate the unemployment (rate). Indeed, the emergence of multinational companies, Unilever for example, provides workforce from different cultural backgrounds with the opportunities to get a decent job on condition that they have a good grasp of English. Thanks to this worldwide language, even people in deprived areas can stand a good chance of leading a comfortably-off life.

Opponents of this idea might maintain that as beneficial as it seems, the expansion of the universal language tongue is a sign of America imperialism, hence posing a potential threat to cultural diversity. They are also convinced that the excessive use of English is the driving force behind the brain drain in various countries. However, I think those thoughts are rather ill-founded because the facts might be the opposite. In reality, international language enables producers in different nations to make their movies become well-known all over the world through the means of English subtitles. Furthermore, had it not been for English, people would not have gained access to a wealth of information, which will contribute to the development of their country.

In conclusion, despite the negative/ detrimental effects English may exert on our lives, I am convinced that the enhancements it brings about are more influential.

330 words

SAMPLE 28

School uniforms should be abolished in all schools.

Discuss what extent do you agree or disagree with this statement.

It is true that school uniforms cause inconvenience to many students. While I admit that may right/ suitable for some people, I trust that in another case, the uniforms are the best solution.

On the one hand, there is a diversity of reasons why schoolchildren are not interested in wearing uniforms. Firstly, uniforms prevent students from showing their personality as well as fashion styles. If students wear uniforms all days of the week, they look similar and quite boring. Secondly, uniforms are expensive so not having to buy them will save money. A full set of uniform has many things: such as shirts, sports clothes, overcoats, and maybe it is unaffordable for many families, especially ones living in poverty/ underprivileged ones.

On the other hand, in some situations, uniforms are the wonderful key. It is time-saving for many students when they do not need to think about what they should wear today. Many schoolgirls, most of them are high school students usually take a lot of time to look beautifully before going out. When uniforms are the only choice, that time can be used more effectively. Moreover, uniforms make students feel equal. It is inevitable that there is the gap between financial resources of students' families. As the result, some of them will wear more costly clothes and bring about discrimination. Last but not least, uniforms also are a great idea to teach discipline.

In conclusion, it is certainly true that uniforms should be rejected to make students' individual stand out, but this is no mean best way for some schools in educating their pupils.

265 words

SAMPLE 29

It is observed that in many countries not enough students are choosing to study science subject.

What are causes? And what will be effects on society?

It is true that the number of science students is becoming inadequate in numerous nations. There are various reasons behind this trend which results in several influences on society.

Students no longer choose science as their major due to two primary causes. First and foremost, those subjects are often challenging, which requires a great deal of patience and intelligence. For example, biology students have to sit in the lab room for a whole day to observe the experimental outcome as well as conduct different researches. Due to such as high level of difficulty and commitment, science subjects have become less attractive to students. Furthermore, there are fewer job prospects in this major compared to business or education field. Hence, learners have a tendency to choose other majors which offer them greater employment opportunities.

Employee shortage in science fields has negative impacts on society as a whole. First of all, when fewer students choose to learn science, the labour force working in this field would be insufficient. Gradually, there would be a significant decrease in the quality of life due to fewer technological inventions. For instance, humans would not be able to produce newer smartphones with better functions. Moreover, the greater participation in other majors such as economics or education certainly leads to the imbalance in the future workforce. In other words, too many degree holders of the same occupation can push a great number of graduates to the verge of unemployment.

In conclusion, demanding requirements of science subjects and a shortage of job opportunities result in fewer students studying these subjects. Consequently, there are serious problems arising from this trend.

270 words

SAMPLE 30

Overpopulation of urban areas has led numerous problems. Identify one or two serious ones and suggest ways that governments and individuals can tackle these problems.

One of the pressing issues that we are facing now is the alarmingly high population density in urban areas. This essay will examine the stumbling block brought by overpopulation and some solutions for this.

There are many problems connected with excessive urban population, one of which is a poor living condition. Living in overpopulated cities, people, especially who have low income, may suffer from the lack of living space. For example, many families in Hong Kong with two or three generations have to cram into just 50m2 apartments. Another issue is the rising level of pollution which can be seen in most populated areas. In fact, the environment is heavily affected by human activities, so places with high density tend to suffer the most from contamination. Last but not least, I personally think that fierce competition among people in crowded cities also needs to be drawn attention. This issue may result in various negative impacts on human life such as relationship damage or stress.

Overpopulation can be tackled by implementing proper measures. Firstly, governments can consider issuing favorable policies that encourage businesses and people to relocate to less populated areas. For example, the government should impose lower tax rate for those who are willing to move out of overcrowded cities. Another possibility is to promote the public transportation in crowded areas to reduce traffic jam and air pollution. Lastly, companies also can make a great contribution by helping to create a friendlier working environment and minimize the stress at work.

In conclusion, there are no easy answers to this challenge but as long as governments and each individual can join hands, it is not impossible to overcome those.

278 words

SAMPLE 31

When new towns are planned, it is more important to include public parks and sports facilities than shopping centers for people to spend their free time in. To what extent do you agree or disagree with this statement?

It is widely argued whether the government should construct/provide more public parks and sports facilities in lieu of shopping malls. While this essay seeks to support this suggestion due to several reasons, some analyses will be also conducted to illustrate the benefits of shopping infrastructure installation in underdeveloped areas.

On the one hand, there are two main explanations why sports centres are indispensable in new town's plan. Firstly, these constructions encourage people to lead a healthy lifestyle. For example, walking around a park not only allows people to enjoy the clean and green atmosphere, but also triggers communication between each other. Secondly, the availability of places to train physically also helps to prevent some young people from wasting too much time and money in shopping malls. Nowadays, young generations tend to be affected by peer's pressure, which urges them to spend dramatically on luxurious clothes, cosmetics, and equipment, in order to show off their wealth to their friends. Thus, the disappearance of shopping centres eliminates the negative influence of following trends on the young.

On the other hand, despite potential drawbacks of shopping expansion, there should be several shopping buildings in new towns. In other words, shopping has played an inevitable role in facilitating the public interest. This is because shopping centres would ease to flavor people's tastes of fashion and domestic products, for instance. Thus, without these stores, many people would miss the chance to catch up with the latest fashion trend as well as cutting-edge technologies. Apart from that, it is, however, believed to contribute considerably to the national fund's development, which would be essential to facilitate other issues of the local living enhancement.

All things considered, a small number of shopping centres should be incorporated in new town's plan, while there should be more places for people to carry out physical activities, so as to create more public areas for leisure and recreation.

316 words

SAMPLE 32

Many people think that the key to mitigating the damage on the environment is by raising fuel's cost. In my opinion, while this is a good option, I believe that there are other measures that could be used to tackle this issue.

On the one hand, there are good reasons why making fuel's price more expensive is the solution to many environmental issues. The high cost of fuels would encourage people to switch to public transport, thus weaken the effect of greenhouse gasses. Specifically, fewer cars on streets mean the lower volume of traffic, which reduces the number of exhaust fumes. In addition, the increase in fuel's price would lead to the shutdown of many oil fields, so less gas would be released into the atmosphere during oil extraction. As a result, pollution and related issues would become less serious compared to the current situation.

On the other hand, people can eliminate environmental problems by employing other choices. The government should impose laws encouraging citizens to protect the environment or to heavily punish those who cause damage to it. Additionally, many campaigns should be organized to raise people's awareness of pollution, therefore discouraging them from worsening the issue. A good example can be seen in Vietnam, where we celebrate Earth Hour by turning off many electronic devices that are unnecessary for an hour, or participating in cleaning streets, schools and workplaces in the weekends.

In conclusion, it is true that increasing the price of fuels is an option to improve the environmental condition, but this is by no means the only solution. Everyone is responsible for protecting our planet before it is too late.

People in all modern societies use drugs, but today's youth are experimenting with both legal and illegal drugs, and at an early age. Some sociologists claim that parents and other members of society often set a bad example.

312 words

SAMPLE 33

Discuss the cause and effects of widespread drug abuse by young people. Make any recommendations you feel are necessary to help fight youth drug abuse.

Nowadays, youth drug abuse has increased at an alarming rate in modern societies which leads to an unhealthy lifestyle. According to some sociologists, parents and other members of society do not set a good role model. There are a number of reasons behind this trend and several solutions should be proposed to solve this problem.

There are two primary reasons why adults set bad examples of using drugs for young folks. The first reason is that teenagers may imitate their idol's bad behaviors because most of the adolescents consider a public figure an ideal person and want to be just like their idol. For instance, Michael Jackson was the drug addict. As a result, the huge number of fans had blind adoration and started to copy his unhealthy lifestyle. Another reason is that in the fast-changing world, some parents pay less attention to their children due to their heavy workload / hectic schedule. Thus, without parent's observation, teenagers would easily become friends with bad people who lead them to unethical behaviors and social crime including abusing illegal drugs.

However, some simple measures should be implemented to deal with the root cause of youth's drug use. Firstly, schools should launch educational campaigns to increase children's perception of drug consumption which could ruin their health and their future by copying their idol's bad behaviors. In addition, the parent should make efforts to take care and give the guidance on how to avoid negative influence from their peers as well as fall in social evils.

In conclusion, the increasing problem of youth drug abuse can be tackled by effective measures in terms of launching campaigns at school and the guidance from parents.

279 words

SAMPLE 34

Many students have to study subjects which they do not like. Some people think this is a complete waste of time. Do you agree or disagree with this statement?

Nowadays, it has been a topic of debate on the fact that students are obliged to study subjects in which they are interested. The main argument for such opinion is that it is a waste of time to do so. However, I completely disagree with this idea.

There is a variety of reasons why pupils should learn all subjects at school, including those they dislike. Firstly, the major target of education is to perfect each person in not only intelligence but also their characteristics and a well-rounded educational and social awareness. Therefore, students will be taught many different subjects in many fields from natural science to social science as well as moral sense. Secondly, skills and knowledge in diversified aspects will help students to be better resulting in reaching a comprehensive education for the future generation. For example, if students only study chemistry and they do not take literature lessons/classes as they hate it, they are sole good at making experiments but they cannot know how to express or write fluently an essay to describe their research on a new invention.

Apart from the practical benefits expressed above, I believe that the time for learning is considerably valuable whether students may join the subject they like or not. As an exploration method for new exciting things around, studying does not mean the lost time for unnecessary work. A student needs knowledge in math to answer a difficult exercise but it is also important for him to learn how to behave reasonably to everyone by moral lessons.

In conclusion, although students may find some subjects not inspiring, they should learn all disciplines/areas/fields equally and seriously because I believe all subjects at school are essential and adequate for students.

287 words

SAMPLE 35

Some people say that relationships should be based on honesty and trust. Others believe that it is sometimes necessary to be dishonest in order to maintain harmony

Which approach do you consider to be better in relationships and why?

Give reasons for your answer and include any relevant examples from your own knowledge or experience.

Honesty and trust play an integral part in guaranteeing a sustainable relationship. I partly agree with this assertion; while it may be true in the majority of cases, others need to be dishonest to keep the close connection.

On the one hand, being honest is a good manner which obviously helps to develop and maintain good relationships in the society. It can benefit those who own this quality considerately. A trustworthy employee, for example, often get quicker progress in job than their counterparts. This is due to the fact that he or she easily gets the belief from his or her own boss. In addition, this manner is an integral part of belief increase in cooperating with partners in the business. Particularly, in most Asian business culture, it is impossible to get a deal if you fail to prove to be a trusted person. In this case, contract papers will consequently be redundant.

On the other hand, in some case, people need to take lie into consideration to maintain good relationships. One reason for this is that telling a white lie could help some people in dealing with difficult situations. My brother, for instance, has just been laid off but he has hidden the truth of his situation from my parents because he thought his problem could make them worry. Another reason is that dishonesty can help people avoid being rude. Since honest people tell a bitter truth about people, they are disregarded among friends, relatives, and colleagues. By way of illustration, if your honest friend straight away speaks about fatal features on your face, you might feel upset and a little offensive.

In conclusion, although I believe people should be honest in their bond, it seems to me that they could sometimes be dishonest to get on well with others.

301 words

SAMPLE 36

In many countries, more and more young people are leaving school but unable to find jobs. What reasons do you think are causing youth unemployment? What measures should be taken to reduce the level of unemployment among youngsters?

It is true that the increase in the unemployment rate among new graduate students is a considerable problem in different parts of the world. There are a variety of possible reasons for this trend, but steps can be definitely taken to mitigate the problem.

In my opinion, three main factors are to blame for the increase in the number of unemployed graduate students. Firstly, the competitiveness in job markets is now witnessing an upward trend with a large number of applicants at different levels of skill. As a result, job seekers who have little or no experience like almost all new graduate students will find it more and more difficult to get a job. Secondly, schools usually have a tendency to focus on academic subjects rather than practical skills such as interpersonal skills or interviewing skills, which is also a vital factor for getting hired. Finally, if students leave schools with neither strong academic records nor sufficient working skills and experience relating to their future job, it is undoubted that they will be unable to meet the requirements of employers.

There are several actions that can be taken to improve this situation. I believe that the change should start with students, who need to do elaborate preparations for their prospective career paths before leaving schools, such as taking part-time jobs or participating in internship programs to acquire more experience in their specialized job fields. Also, schools ought to empower their young students by adding a training course of practical skills and job orientation programs to their curriculums. At the same time, Governments should try to increase the field of jobs in every sector, which encourage and open up opportunities for self-employment.

In conclusion, the unemployment rate among youngsters may continue to rise unless adolescents, schools, and governments take prudent steps to tackle this problem.

304 words

SAMPLE 37

Problems with environmental pollution have become so serious that many countries are trying to solve these problems. What are causes and how could they be reduced?

It is true that many nations are attempting to address serious environmental pollution problems today. There are various reasons behind this issue and several solutions should be proposed to mitigate this trend.

There is no doubt that human activities are the main reason why environmental pollution problems have become serious. Firstly, it can have an adverse impact on the air because everyday people have to use fossil fuels by burning them in order to meet basic human needs such as traveling and lighting. Therefore, the large amount of CO_2 and other heat-trapping gases is released into the atmosphere. Secondly, as the population grows, the demand for housing will also increase rapidly. As a result, people have to deforest as much as possible to build their houses. This could cause the soil pollution and flood when it rains.

However, people also can take steps to address the problems described above. One of the most potential/plausible solutions would be to encourage citizens to use the sustainable energy sources such as solar energy. For example, in the United State, people are recommended by the government to buy the cars which use solar energy instead of petrol. Consequently, the amount of CO_2 emissions is reduced considerably. Another measure is that government should encourage people to live in the public buildings rather than in the private houses. This can help save the forest and people have much more land to plant a tree.

In conclusion, various measures can be taken to tackle the serious environmental pollution problems that many countries are facing.

257 words

SAMPLE 38

Putting criminals into prisons is not an effective way to deal with them. Instead, education and job training should be offered. To what extent do you agree or disagree?

People have different views about the methods to handle criminals. While I accept that jail sentences are effective in some countries, I believe that the authorities should have alternative measures to punish the offenders.

Firstly, it is clear that sending all inmates to prisons is a waste of time and public funds. Nowadays, prisoners are often provided with luxuries such as the internet, TVs, and delicacies, which are paid by other citizens. For example, those who are in the jail Beveren in Belgium are allowed to play video games, surf the Net and watch movies all day long. As a result, law-breakers can get a satisfaction in psychology at taxpayers' expense and thus, lead to injustice.

Moreover, the main purpose of punishing somebody is to change their behavior, which will not be obtained by sending them to jail. This is because, most of them, when sitting in a goal and are not provided with education, will think about committing another crime. For instance, if a theft has to be confined to a murderer, he may be inspired and imitate the killer's action. Therefore, propaganda and job training can be a preventive measure for him.

This is not to say that we should always be lenient on criminals, especially the serious ones. Imprisoning them helps protect the victims. However, during their punishment, they should have a chance to learn job-related skills, soft skills, and even pure knowledge. Only by doing so can we meet the aim of preventing illegal behaviors from happening again and sending a strong message to would-be criminals.

In conclusion, although putting law-breakers to prison is a good means of stopping offences, the main method should be educating and career training in order to get a deterrent effect.

289 words

SAMPLE 39

The government should ban smoking in all public places, even though this would restrict some other people's freedoms.

Do you agree or disagree?

Give reasons for your answer.

Currently, public smoking has been an alarming social problem and there was an opinion in the society suggesting that the authorities should forbid it. Personally, I strongly support this idea although it could raise a concern about committing individual freedoms. The essay hereby will express my reasons.

First and foremost, we all feel it in our bones that smoking is detrimental to our health and it is more likely to be effective on the passive smokers, which are the people surrounding the direct smokers. Observed in Vietnam, in 2010, smoking was one of the most prominent causes of death just after vehicle accidents, as analyzed, tobacco resulted in 22% of the male death toll and 9.5% of the female death toll. In the ensuing years, these percentages have dropped dramatically on account of public smoking restriction. So this ban was executed for the sake of our health.

Second of all, it is not rocket science to perceive that personal cut on cigarette helps us save our budget from purchasing this commodity as well as paying for medicine, health care against its impairment. My uncle's situation is a good case in point. He used to be a cigarette heavy-addicted person and now he has been treated lengthily in a hospital with an accumulated cost estimated an arm and a leg.

In conclusion, smoking is one of the most outstanding social disasters. In my perspective, the practice of forbidding smoking in public is an essential policy and should be multiplied more in the society.

252 words

SAMPLE 40

Countries are becoming more and more similar because people are able to buy the same products anywhere in the world.

Do you think this is a positive or negative development?

Nowadays, since people in different countries can purchase the same goods and services, it is often claimed that all nations are a lot more similar than ever before. This trend, in my opinion, presents both benefits and drawbacks.

On the one hand, that many people in the world are using the same products is considered part of globalization. When this phenomenon happens, more and more international corporations start to enter domestic markets by opening more outlets, agencies in other countries. This convenience will enable customers to buy their favorite products from many brands without going out of their home countries. For example, Toyota is a well-known car company which has opened many outlets in India and this allows Indians to buy branded cars more easily without going to Japan. Furthermore, tourists who are difficult to adapt to new adjustments find it uncomfortable to be exposed to new products. Therefore, it would be easier for travelers to go abroad and find products or services that they often use at home.

On the other hand, this development may pose a threat to the diversity of local businesses and cultures. Due to a great deal of exposure to foreign products of higher quality as well as affordable price, consumers have a tendency to turn their backs on local products. Consequently, many small local companies would not sustain their business in the long run and the worst case is that their business may be shut down for being incapable of competing with international companies. Moreover, the disappearance of these local businesses would cause a big loss to the local cultures. Hence, using home products is one of the best ways to maintain the national culture and cultural loss would not occur if domestic consumption should be encouraged.

In conclusion, although there are some pros and cons in this development, it is better for us not to let its disadvantages overshadow advantages so that this trend can make a contribution to bettering people's lives.

329 words

SAMPLE 41

With the rise of eBooks comes the decline in paper books. Some people see this as a good forward step while others do not.

What are advantages and disadvantages of this trend?

It is believed that paper books will be replaced and eBooks are becoming the wave of the future. While some people consider the popularity of eBooks as a positive trend, others do not. This essay will analyze the benefits of reading books online as well as the drawbacks of this trend, followed by a reasoned conclusion.

On the one hand, eBooks have brought significant benefits compared to paper counterparts when it comes to convenience and lower prices. Firstly, people can enjoy online reading anytime anywhere with smartphones or hand-held electric devices while printed books not only occupy much more space on bookshelves but also are hard to carry. Secondly, it would be much cheaper to buy eBooks as various offers are often available on the Internet with attractive discounts and no shipping costs. For example, Amazon, which is currently one of the largest e-commerce platforms, attracts thousands of eBook orders every day from all over the world.

On the other hand, there are some inevitable drawbacks that associate with the overuse of eBooks and e-readers. Spending too much time staring at the screen may lead to a headache and eyestrain which can pose threats to physical health in the long term. Moreover, e-readers or electric devices are made from plastics and heavy metals that are not good for the environment and are worse than paper. For example, a red warning has recently alarmed that the increasing production of electric devices including e-readers can cause severe damage to the environment.

In conclusion, the merits and demerits of this trend are numerous. However, after analyzing both sides, in my view, reading e-books are more advantageous than reading paper books. Hence, it is believed that in years to come, the world would see a rapid rise in their sales.

296 words

SAMPLE 42

Some people believe the government should spend money on building train and subway lines to reduce traffic congestion. Others think that building more and wider roads is the better way to reduce traffic congestion. Discuss both views and give your opinion.

It is true that the problem of traffic jams has become increasingly serious. While some people believe that funds should be allocated to expanding and improving road system to tackle this problem, I think that in order to address such issue, money from governments should go to the construction of rail and subway networks.

On the one hand, there are two reasons why it is believed that building and widening roads would be much more efficient. The first reason is that the existing roads are now inadequate to deal with the increasing number of cars. As a consequence of urban sprawl, many staff members now have to commute from the suburbs to the inner city for work by using their cars, so the new road routes and broad avenues must be created to handle the growing volume of traffic. Secondly, because, even outside the cities, there is also growing traffic congestion, building more interstate roads is needed to allow people to reach their destination without facing the problem.

On the other hand, I would consider that the construction of metro lines and rail would be the best solution to the problems of traffic congestion. Firstly, Thanks to these means of transport, they might travel more quickly and safely to their workplace. As a result, investment and funding for infrastructure in the form of high-capacity public transport would encourage people to shift from their private vehicles to rail and metro services. This will relieve pressure on existing networks. Secondly, it is sometimes impossible to build more roads or increase road space, especially in the major cities. As land is rarely available to enable such development to take place, the construction of metro networks would be a more practical option.

In conclusion, although widening and building more roads can alleviate traffic congestion, it seems to me that in order to solve the root causes of traffic congestion, constructing rapid transit lines would be the best decision.

324 words

SAMPLE 43

Whether or not someone achieves their aims is mostly by a question of luck. To what extent do you agree or disagree?

Many people have different views about what elements contribute mostly to a person's success. While I accept that luck is an indispensable factor that helps people to reach their goals, I believe that hard work and determination will have more impact on an individual.

On the one hand, luck is only a small factor in determining one's achievement. Firstly, people cannot be dependent on luck to become successful. If students want to pass the exam with a high mark, they have to burn the midnight oil for their study. If not, chances are he or she will fail, no matter how lucky he or she may be. Secondly, luck could only lead people to short-term achievement and there is nothing to ascertain that it would continue to exist in the long run. The over-reliance on good fortune would prevent people from achieving their long-term or long-life aims.

On the other hand, I believe that determined and industrious people will be successful in whatever they do. Hard-working people usually attain their goals. For example, before becoming one of the best football players in the world, David Beckham had to go through intense training hours every day for many years. Another clear case of success through determination is Nguyen Ngoc Ky, a disabled man who cannot write by hand, but he was determined enough to teach himself to write by foot. He became one of the greatest teachers in the history of education in Vietnam and was a typical role model for the young generation to follow.

In conclusion, while I agree that luck contributes to one's success, I believe that only determination and hard work are the most important factors.

279 words

SAMPLE 44

The internet has transformed the way information is shared and consumed, but it has also created problems that did not exist before. What are the most serious problems associated with the internet and what solutions can you suggest?

It is not deniable that the internet plays an indispensable part in our lives nowadays. Although there are undoubtedly some negative consequences of this source, people should take steps to mitigate these potential problems.

In my opinion, several related problems can be anticipated when the internet has been developed. One main problem lies in the internet fraud when someone steals user's information or personal identity. For example, a criminal can access a bank account or business transaction by a stolen account. Equally important, people may be negatively affected when accessing dangerous online sites. Especially, children are vulnerable to bad behaviours such as violent or sedentary lifestyle after surfing non-educational websites. Besides, the internet may widen the gap between family members. The virtual life in the websites seems to make people no longer be responsible for their real families.

However, people could take several actions to solve the mentioned problems. Firstly, the government should impose strict regulations to control illegal activities of internet crime as well as spend money on upgrading the online security system. Secondly, people need to raise awareness about drawbacks and risky problems of the internet. Banks and businesses need to warn their customers of the potential consequences of stealing personal identity, instructing them how to prevent these risks. Finally, in each family, not only parents have to set a role model but they also should play their parts in monitoring their children's activities.

In conclusion, the internet always contains potential negative outcomes; the government and residents can set clear rules and effective measures to tackle these problems.

260 words

SAMPLE 45

Today, more school leavers are unable to find jobs. Discuss the causes of rising unemployment among young adults and suggest any solutions.

The 21st-century job market has become more competitive than ever before due to the transformational shift from manufacturing society into a heavy knowledge-based society. These changes have hugely impacted the possibilities to secure decent jobs for school leavers. Two major causes for the rising unemployment among young adults can be identified as the exponential surge in the number of higher education graduates at a global scale and the lightning speed of modern technology development which results in automatic alternatives for most low-skilled works. These factors will be discussed in more details, followed by some solutions for this troubling issue.

Recent sociology studies have proven that university and higher education participation rate grows in tandem with the improvement of living standards in most parts of the world. When students from the university and above levels join the job market, they certainly make the under-graduates become less desirable talent sources in almost every job aspect and industry. Furthermore, as more and more robots are introduced into the workforce to take charge of simple and manual responsibilities, school leavers even have to face fiercer competition with not only people, but machines which do not require numeral labor benefits as a human job seeker does. Take Japan for example. While most of the cleaning and delivery jobs are well-taken care by excellently programmed auto systems, low skilled workers have hard times finding such kinds of jobs. Thus, the increasing number of unemployed high-school students is a natural result of these demand-supply mechanics.

The most effective solution for this unhealthy social and economic issue should be introducing financial and academic supports to encourage school leavers to pursue higher education. This can promise them better opportunities to nail their dream jobs and reduce the chances of becoming potentially jobless. Career consultation officers would also need to work more diligently to give young students valuable advice on what major to take in after high school graduation. The teenagers themselves need to be more active in thinking & planning their future career from early stages of the inspiration and guidance from their parents.

As suggested above, while the unemployment rate among under-graduates is an uptrend, there are possible ways to reverse the situation. Governments, schools & family orientations, therefore, play big roles in facilitating career securities for young job seekers.

382 words

SAMPLE 46

The world natural resources are being consumed at an ever-increased rate. What are the dangers of this situation? What should we do?

It is true that the consumption of natural resources has been increasing at a dangerous rate. This results in a number of drawbacks for the lives of people and animals; therefore, effective methods should be applied to deal with these problems.

In these days, the lives of people and all species have suffered from negative consequences due to overconsumption of natural resources. The first one is that more and more species such as tigers and elephants are on the verge of extinction due to the loss of natural habitats and illegal hunting. For example, trees are being cut down, and wild animals are dying out to due to the construction of industrial sites, food, and medical manufacturers. Secondly, people have to encounter natural disasters more frequently due to the loss of rainforests. For instance, soil erosions, as well as floods, have cost the lives of millions of people and their assets annually, and these need many years to recover.

To resolve these problems, feasible measures should be adopted. The first method is that there should be more programmes about the roles and conditions of natural resources on mass media. By this way, people's awareness would be raised, and they could mitigate these adverse problems by using energy more economically. In addition, in schools and companies, people should be encouraged to take part in activities to protect the natural environment. These programmes such as Earth Hour and planting trees can reduce negative effects that overconsumption has brought.

In conclusion, excessively exploiting natural resources can cause a number of negative effects, but these problems can be mitigated by feasible activities.

268 words

SAMPLE 47

The gap between the rich and the poor is increasingly wide, as rich people become richer and poor people grow poorer. What problems could this situation cause? What are the solutions to address those problems?

It is undeniable that the disparity between rich people and poor people becomes wider. The phenomenon causes several serious issues for society, and solutions should be proposed to deal with the matter.

To begin with, there are some issues that will happen if the inequality between the rich and the poor keeps growing. First of all, the number of crime rate will rise significantly. Obviously, living in poverty is the main reason forcing many people to commit offences to make money which may support them to afford their basic needs. Furthermore, some of the human rights are unable to be protected effectively. Child abuse is a clear illustration when many disadvantaged children have to work under the age of eighteen to assist their families in financial issues. As they are still too young, they are unlikely to protect themselves from being exploited by their employers, leading to many adverse impacts on both mental and physical development of the children.

However, measures should be taken immediately to minimize the gap between the wealthy and the poor. First, governments should apply tax policies in which those who are well off should pay a higher tax. By doing this, the national budgets may become larger, which in turns being allocated to support the citizens in need. As a result, impoverished children are unlikely to earn money thanks to the government subsidies. Second, authorities should help create more employment opportunities for the needy. For instance, governments can establish more vocational schools which provide disadvantaged people with free job training programs. This practice could help the needy find jobs to solve their financial problems instead of stealing things from others.

In conclusion, it is clear that there are numerous issues caused by the economic inequality between the rich and the poor, and steps should be taken to narrow the gap.

305 words

CONCLUSION

Thank you again for downloading this book on *"IELTS Writing Task 2 Samples: Over 45 High-Quality Model Essays for Your Reference to Gain a High Band Score 8.0+ In 1 Week (Book 13)."* and reading all the way to the end. I'm extremely grateful.

If you know of anyone else who may benefit from the useful task 2 writing sample essays for their reference, please help me inform them of this book. I would greatly appreciate it.

Finally, if you enjoyed this book and feel that it has added value to your work and study in any way, please take a couple of minutes to share your thoughts and post a REVIEW on Amazon. Your feedback will help me to continue to write other books of IELTS topic that helps you get the best results. Furthermore, if you write a simple REVIEW with positive words for this book on Amazon, you can help hundreds or perhaps thousands of other readers who may want to improve their English writing skills sounding like a native speaker. Like you, they worked hard for every penny they spend on books. With the information and recommendation you provide, they would be more likely to take action right away. We really look forward to reading your review.

Thanks again for your support and good luck!

If you enjoy my book, please write a POSITIVE REVIEW on Amazon.

-- Rachel Mitchell --

CHECK OUT OTHER BOOKS

Go here to check out other related books that might interest you:

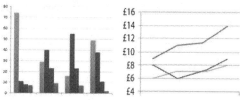

Ielts Academic Writing Task 1 Samples : Over 35 High Quality Samples for Your Reference to Gain a High Band Score 8.0+ In 1 Week (Book 1)

https://www.amazon.com/dp/B076V62DZC

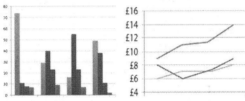

Ielts Academic Writing Task 1 Samples : Over 35 High Quality
Samples for Your Reference to Gain a High Band Score 8.0+ In 1
Week (Book 2)

https://www.amazon.com/dp/B076VDY58V

Shortcut To English Collocations: Master 2000+ English Collocations In Used Explained Under 20 Minutes A Day (5 books in 1 Box set)

https://www.amazon.com/dp/B06W2P6S22

IELTS Writing Task 1 + 2: The Ultimate Guide with Practice to Get a Target Band Score of 8.0+ In 10 Minutes a Day

https://www.amazon.com/dp/B075DFYPG6

IELTS Speaking Strategies: The Ultimate Guide With Tips, Tricks, And Practice On How To Get A Target Band Score Of 8.0+ In 10 Minutes A Day.

https://www.amazon.com/dp/B075JCW65G

Shortcut To Ielts Writing: The Ultimate Guide To Immediately Increase Your Ielts Writing Scores.

https://www.amazon.com/dp/B01JV7EQGG

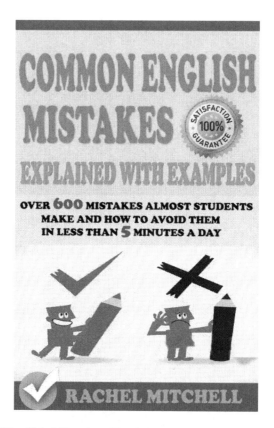

Common English Mistakes Explained With Examples: Over 600
Mistakes Almost Students Make and How to Avoid Them in Less
Than 5 Minutes A Day

https://www.amazon.com/dp/B072PXVHNZ

Paraphrasing Strategies: 10 Simple Techniques For Effective Paraphrasing In 5 Minutes Or Less

https://www.amazon.com/dp/B071DFG27Q

Legal Vocabulary In Use: Master 600+ Essential Legal Terms And Phrases Explained In 10 Minutes A Day

http://www.amazon.com/dp/B01L0FKXPU

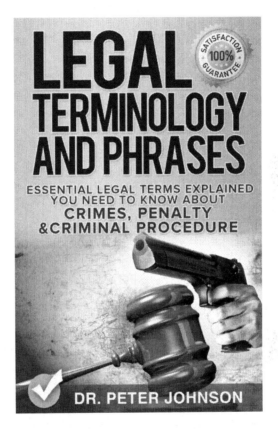

Legal Terminology And Phrases: Essential Legal Terms Explained You Need To Know About Crimes, Penalty And Criminal Procedure

http://www.amazon.com/dp/B01L5EB54Y

Productivity Secrets For Students: The Ultimate Guide To Improve Your Mental Concentration, Kill Procrastination, Boost Memory And Maximize Productivity In Study

http://www.amazon.com/dp/B01JS52UT6

Daughter of Strife: 7 Techniques On How To Win Back Your Stubborn Teenage Daughter

https://www.amazon.com/dp/B01HS5E3V6

Parenting Teens With Love And Logic: A Survival Guide To Overcoming The Barriers Of Adolescence About Dating, Sex And Substance Abuse

https://www.amazon.com/dp/B01JQUTNPM

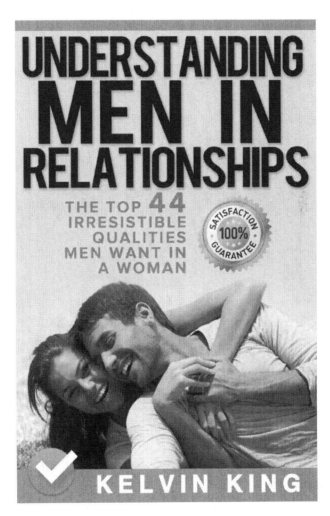

http://www.amazon.com/dp/B01K0ARNA4

Made in the USA
San Bernardino, CA
10 December 2018